From the Heart with Tears

PLAN AND DELIVER A HEARTFELT EULOGY

Kaylene Ledgar

First published by Ultimate World Publishing 2019
Copyright © 2019 Kaylene Ledgar

ISBN
Paperback - 978-1-925884-67-8
Ebook - 978-1-925884-68-5

Kaylene Ledgar has asserted her right under the Copyright, Designs and Patents Act 1988 to be identified as the author of this work. The information in this book is based on the author's experiences and opinions. The publisher specifically disclaims responsibility for any adverse consequences, which may result from use of the information contained herein. Permission to use information has been sought by the author. Any breaches will be rectified in further editions of the book.

All rights reserved. No part of this publication may be reproduced, stored in or introduced into a retrieval system, or transmitted in any form, or by any means (electronic, mechanical, photocopying, recording or otherwise) without the prior written permission of the author. Any person who does any unauthorised act in relation to this publication may be liable to criminal prosecution and civil claims for damages. Enquiries should be made through the publisher.

Cover design: Ultimate World Publishing
Layout and typesetting: Ultimate World Publishing
Editor: James Salmon

Ultimate World Publishing
Diamond Creek,
Victoria Australia 3089
www.writeabook.com.au

Dedication

*To the special people who say "yes" to deliver a eulogy,
this book is for you, from my heart with tears.*

From the Heart with Tears

Contents

Dedication iii

Introduction 1

Chapter 1: Saying "Yes" 5

Chapter 2: Getting started 9

Chapter 3: Right package 21

Chapter 4: Bringing it all together 29

Chapter 5: Finding Inspiration 39

Afterword 43

About the author 45

From the Heart with Tears

Introduction

Grief is the price we pay for love.
QUEEN ELIZABETH II

As I write this book, the loss of my dad earlier this year is still very raw. The memory of having to prepare and deliver the eulogy at his celebration of life has inspired me to write this book.

From the Heart with Tears, this is my gift to the special people who have the tremendous honour of paying tribute to a loved one who has passed. In most cases there are only a few days from when you are asked to give a eulogy and when you deliver it.

Having delivered four eulogies and coached others to create and deliver eulogies, I have created a simple process to help you prepare and deliver a tribute worthy of your loved one. This book is designed to help you pull together a eulogy, with confidence, in a few days.

The process I share to help you with preparing and delivering a eulogy can be adapted for other celebration speeches.

FREE Resource

Visit www.kayleneledgar.com.au/eulogywb to download your FREE copy of:

- From the Heart with Tears workbook for preparing a eulogy. You can use this to prepare any celebration style speech.

From the Heart with Tears

CHAPTER 1

Saying "Yes"

It is during our darkest moments that we must focus to see the light.
ARISTOTLE

✦ ✦ ✦

The most difficult, yet most important speeches of my life have been the tributes for those that have passed.

I was first asked to give my grandparents' eulogies following a two-minute toast that I presented at my grandad's 80th birthday party. As soon I had finished, my grandma turned to me and said, "You can do my eulogy." Quickly followed by Grandad, "You can do mine too." I was surprised and honoured at the same time. Both were in good health and the thought of funerals were far from my mind. Looking at them, loving them, how could I refuse? I agreed to do their eulogies.

When I told Darling, my dad's mum, about this, she liked the idea and asked me to do her eulogy too. Since then, I have delivered the eulogy for Grandad and Darling. I delivered a eulogy at a friend's funeral and helped another friend prepare a eulogy for a mutual friend. When my dad was diagnosed with stage 4 cancer late in 2018, he didn't ask me to give his eulogy, he just knew I would. In Dad's final weeks, I was asked if I thought I would be ok to deliver the eulogy and I simply said, "I have to, he is my dad, I will do it for him and I will do it for the family." Early in 2019, 13 weeks after Dad was diagnosed, I stood in front of my family and friends, grieving the greatest loss of my life, as I delivered the speech of my life, my dad's eulogy.

In times of grief, if I can make it easier for the family and for the friends, I will stand up and I will do the eulogy. Honouring the life of a loved one is difficult, but when faced with grief, the fear of speaking is less painful than the loss. Standing up while consumed with grief and speaking is not easy, whether you are doing it for the first time or you have done it before.

Delivering a eulogy is difficult even when you are a confident speaker. If you fear speaking, your automatic response when asked to deliver a eulogy is likely to be "no". You may find yourself saying:

> Why would I want to put myself in that position?
>
> Why do something I fear?
>
> What if I make a mistake?
>
> I'm grieving, I just can't do it.

From my experience, when we shift our focus from "I" and focus on the family, you just have to say "yes" when asked. The family asked you to give the eulogy for a reason, they could have asked another but they chose you. They believe you are the right person for this important role. Trust their judgement that you are the right person for this special job.

When you deliver a eulogy, you speak from your heart, you respectfully honour the person and provide comfort to the family and mourners. With the focus on the person you are honouring and their loved ones, you shift the focus away from you, and you can rise above your fear.

A final word on saying yes

Saying yes is difficult to do however the gift you are providing to the family and loved ones is something they will cherish forever.

CHAPTER 2

Getting started

To live in hearts we leave behind is not to die.
THOMAS CAMPBELL

You have said "yes", you will deliver the eulogy, but where do you start?

Like with any speech, you want to do your homework before you start creating the speech. The getting started door is where you unlock information about the service, clarify expectations of family and identify key information about the person you will be honouring.

Information about the service

To help you prepare for the eulogy you will want to know details about the service including:

o   When and where will the service be held?

o   How long is allocated for the eulogy?

o   Who will be leading the service?

o   Will there be other speakers or tributes?

At the time of being asked to deliver the eulogy, some of the details about the service may not be available. Without this information you can continue preparing.

The time allocated for the eulogy varies. I have had from as little as five minutes to as long as 18 minutes. If the timing is unknown when you start preparing your speech, I would focus on preparing a five-minute eulogy. It is easier to add more content if you are allowed more time.

Clarifying the expectations of family

While the eulogy is about the person being honoured, it is important to clarify expectations with the family. They, as you are, will be grieving. Grief takes on many forms and we all grieve differently. Early days of grief are often filled with shock and sadness, so it can be difficult for family members to know what they want from the eulogy. This is where you may need to guide them by asking a few questions:

- o Is there anything you do not want me to include in the eulogy?

- o Is there anything you specifically want me to include?

- o I will come up with a plan for the eulogy, would you like me to share that with you before I start writing the eulogy?

o Are their people that you would like me to talk to who might have stories or insights that I might be able to use in the eulogy?

o Is there anyone you would like me to acknowledge or thank when I deliver the eulogy?

Identify key information

To uncover key information about the person being honoured spend time with family members and friends. Listen to their stories and make notes. Capture details, keywords and phrases. Share your memories and stories with the family and add them to your notes.

You want to gather information that will help define the character, the heart of the person. What made this person unique? What made people love them? You want to capture stories and insights that will remind those grieving of the wonderful life their loved one lived.

The eulogy is about the person, not about you and not just about your relationship with them. That said, I feel it is important that you do share what they meant to you and your own personal insights.

Here is a guide of the type of information you can gather:

- o Personal details

    - What was their full name?
    - Did they have any nicknames?
    - When and where were they born?
    - When did they pass away?

- o Early years

    - Who were their parents?
    - Did they have any siblings? If yes, what are their names?
    - Where did they go to school?
    - Did they have any significant education or other achievements while at school?
    - What were their interests as a child and teenager?
    - What did they want to be or do when they grew up?

- Family

  - Did they have a partner? If yes, who are they and when did they meet?
  - Did they have children, grandchildren/great grandchildren? If yes, who are they?
  - What are some of the beautiful memories about their time together?
  - What is something the loved ones will miss about the person?

- Career, business

  - What did they do for a living?
  - Who did they work for?
  - What was their role?
  - Did they have any significant career achievements?

- Hobbies and interests

  - Were they a member of any clubs?
  - Did they have a favourite sports team?
  - What did they enjoy doing?
  - How did they spend most of their time?
  - What was their favourite pastime?

In their words

To be able to speak the words of the person you are honouring provides a special moment for all.

If you know in advance that you will be asked to deliver a eulogy, you can gather information directly. Encourage them to talk and share their stories, ask them questions and take notes. If you can, ask them to sum up their life.

When I asked my dad about his life, his message was clear: "I have no regrets." Dad, knowing his time was limited, was very clear on what he wanted me to share with people. He wanted to specifically thank people for their contribution to his amazing life. I shared his words, his thank you at the service, I spoke his words when he no longer could.

You may want to start a journal, capturing special moments in your life and the lives of those you love. You never know when you may be called upon to speak and having a journal of stories will make it easier for you to prepare the speech or eulogy.

Action: Let's get started.

Prepare for the eulogy by answering the following sets of questions.

Information about the service

When and where will the service be held?

How long is allocated for the eulogy?

Who will be leading the service?

Will there be other speakers or tributes?

Expectations of the family

Is there anything you do not want me to include in the eulogy?

Is there anything you specifically want me to include?

I will come up with a plan for the eulogy, would you like me to share that with you before I start writing the eulogy?

Are their people that you would like me to talk to who might have stories or insights that I might be able to use in the eulogy?

Is there anyone you would like me to acknowledge or thank when I deliver the eulogy?

Action: Identify key information.

Gather key information using the following sets of questions:

Personal details

What was their full name?

Did they have any nicknames?

When and where were they born?

When did they pass away?

Early years

Who were their parents?

Did they have any siblings? If yes, what are their names?

Where did they go to school?

Did they have any significant education or other achievements while at school?

What were their interests as a child and teenager?

What did they want to be or do when they grew up?

Family

Did they have a partner? If yes, who are they and when did they meet?

Did they have children, grandchildren/great grandchildren? If yes, who are they?

What are some of the beautiful memories about their time together?

What is something the loved ones will miss about the person?

Career, business

What did they do for a living?

Who did they work for?

What was their role?

Did they have any significant career achievements?

Hobbies and interests

Were they a member of any clubs?

Did they have a favourite sports team?

What did they enjoy doing?

How did they spend most of their time?

What was their favourite pastime?

A final word on getting started

You don't have to do this alone, draw on those close to the person you are honouring, they will help you find the words.

CHAPTER 3

Right package

Say not in grief: "He is no more",
but live in thankfulness that he was.
HEBREW PROVERB

✦ ✦ ✦

Having gathered key information and listened to many stories, you then need to decide what will be included in the eulogy. It is likely that you have enough stories to fill a book, which means you will need to carefully select what you can realistically cover in the eulogy.

The first part of the right package door is turning key points into a structure, and the second part is writing the eulogy in full.

Turning key points into a structure

Firstly, review all of your notes and identify 3 to 5 key themes – this will be body of your eulogy. The key themes may be early years, family, career and interests.

In addition to the body of the eulogy, you will have an opening and a conclusion.

The opening is where you can introduce yourself if the person leading the service has not introduced you and your relationship to the person being honoured. In the opening, you will introduce the person you are honouring.

The conclusion is where you share the person's own words. Your final words should highlight the essence of the person and the mark they have left on this world.

You may also want to include a thank you for people who have travelled a distanced to be there or to medical staff or others. In my dad's eulogy I acknowledged the oncologists and nursing staff at the hospital. I also acknowledged the support of my dad's sister-in-law, my aunt Sharen, who worked at the hospital and was there every step of the way looking after Dad and the family. Let the family guide who you should acknowledge and thank. You do not want to be thanking by name a lot of people – thank key people by name only, then offer a more general thank you.

If you are not a family member, you may want to offer your condolences to the family before your final words.

Here is a sample outline for a eulogy:

- o Opening, introduce yourself and the person you are honouring.

- o Early years, parents, siblings, schooling.

- o Family, their partner, children, grandchildren.

- o Career, what they did for a living.

- o Interests, sports, activities they were into.

- Thank you to key people.

- Conclusion, condolences to the family, a final word about the person and the mark they have left.

Using the sample outline with five minutes allocated for the eulogy, you will have approximately 50 seconds for each of the key themes and 50 seconds for the opening and conclusion combined. You may decide that you want to allocate more time to one key theme over another. That is fine, there is no rule that says you have to allocate each key theme the same amount of time. You may choose to allocate more time to interests, taking it to 90 seconds, and less time to career and thank you, dropping them to 30 seconds each.

I speak on average 135 words per minute, so for a five-minute speech that is approximately 675 words. If you want to you can work out your average words per minute – time yourself as you read out loud. Divide the total words read by the time it took, and this will give you your average words per minute.

Writing the eulogy

Now that you have your outline, it is time to start writing the eulogy. Finding the right words can be hard. I recommend that when you begin try to write and not think about the actual words. You can review and edit when you have the initial draft captured.

Sometimes it is easier to speak out the eulogy using voice to text software. If you choose to do this, use the structure that you prepared as a guide and simply talk out each of the parts. As with when you write out the eulogy, don't worry about saying the right words, just capture your words, then review and edit later.

Don't think that you have to find all the words for the eulogy yourself. You spent time with the family and friends, you listened to their stories, they gave you the words and you can use them. I feel by using the words of others in the eulogy, it provides a small comfort to them. It makes the moment extra special for them as they know their special moment is being shared.

Stories are powerful, they evoke memories and help drive home key points. A simple technique to illustrate your key themes in the eulogy is to tell a story, then make a point. I have also done the reverse for eulogies, making the point then sharing a story.

In the time allocated, you can't share everything, therefore selecting stories that will demonstrate the point is better than providing a shopping list of attributes and achievements.

Once you have written or spoken the draft eulogy, take a break, grab a cuppa, go for a walk, clear your mind, then come back with a clear head to review and edit. As you review, look for opportunities to tighten the content without losing the message. If you find that in the draft you are using an adjective repeatedly, you may want to use the thesaurus function to find a different word.

As you practice the eulogy, you can continue to make changes. I have been known to make changes right up till the moment I stand to deliver the eulogy.

Action: Create the right package.

Select the key themes for the eulogy and create an outline for the eulogy.

Opening:

Key theme 1:

Key theme 2:

Key theme 3:

Thank you:

Conclusion:

Action: Write the eulogy.

Using the outline write the eulogy. You may elect to speak out the eulogy using voice to text software.

Review and edit the draft eulogy.

A final word on the right package

Take time to find the right package and right stories – in the case of a eulogy, less is more.

CHAPTER 4

Bringing it all together

What we once enjoyed and deeply loved we can never lose, for all that we love deeply becomes part of us.
HELEN KELLER

✦ ✦ ✦

As you bring it all together, make sure you take care of yourself and work through your own feelings of grief.

Practice reading the eulogy out loud

Due to the short time frame, you will want to jump right in and start practicing as you plan to deliver the eulogy. That means practice with your notes the way they will be printed on the day.

Here are my tips for using notes:

- Use large font. The font should be easily read from a standing position if you drop the page on the floor. I used to recommend Arial 22 point however as my eyes are getting old, this does not work for me. Find the font size that works best for you.

- Use double spacing or 1 ½ spacing. This will give you room to make changes in pen and makes it easier to see the words.

- Start each sentence on a new line.

- Add an extra line between paragraphs. This will help you pause, breathe and continue while filled with emotions.

- Number each of the pages.

- Print single sided.

- Place all pages on the right-hand side of the lectern.

- As you near the end of the page, slowly move the page to the left. Doing this will allow you to move to the top of the next page easily.

- As you read your speech, lift your eyes regularly to make contact with the audience.

- Use your finger as a guide – this will help you easily find your place when your eyes return to the script.

- Practice reading the speech and lifting your eyes. If you can do it in front of a mirror, do so, as this way you can lift your eyes, make eye contact with yourself, before looking back at the script. The more you practice the easier it will be to read the script and make eye contact with the audience.

If you are worried about your nerves or emotions getting the better of you, consider putting a prompt on each page top right-hand corner to help you maintain focus. To help me stay focused I would consider using a red heart, a symbol of love or a sunflower, a symbol to stand tall and proud or a smiley face, a symbol to prompt me to smile.

As you practice, make any necessary changes. If you find you are stumbling over a word, consider changing it. If you find particular words hard to deliver, is there another way you can phrase it that is easier to say? For me, when I delivered my dad's eulogy, I referred to him mostly as David because referring to him as Dad simply hurt too much and I knew I would struggle to hold it together. Using David throughout the eulogy meant that when I was sharing my own words, the words from my heart, I could say Dad and while it hurt, I managed. Sharing stories from others helped, because I could focus on the person whose story I was sharing and it gave me strength.

Time yourself reading the eulogy out loud a few times to ensure that you will be within the allocated time. If you are consistently taking longer than allocated to read the eulogy, consider where you can remove or tighten up some content. A story that is four or more sentences may need to be shortened to two or three sentences.

Delivering the eulogy

On the day, make sure you pack your notes, water at room temperate – not icy cold – and a small packet of tissues. If you can, arrive early and introduce yourself to the person leading the service. Confirm how and when you will be introduced. Take a moment to gather yourself. It can be quite confronting walking in and seeing the coffin or photos for the first time. Familiarise yourself with the area where you will be speaking from. Stand behind the lectern and look at the room. Secure a seat that will allow you to easily make your way to the lectern. Take a few moments for yourself before speaking to family and other guests.

Take your seat along with the other mourners. As it nears the time for you to deliver the eulogy, it may help to do a deep breathing exercise where you breathe in for the count of three, hold for the count of three and exhale to the count of three. Taking a small sip of water can help calm the nerves. Remember as you stand to walk to the lectern, the family asked you to do this, they believe in you, you are doing this for the person you are honouring and their family. You have practiced and you are ready.

While delivering the eulogy, you may have tears – let them flow. If the emotion starts to impact on your voice or you feel that you are about to break, pause and take a deep breath before continuing. You are allowed to take that moment to gather yourself before you move on – this will also give the attendees a moment to gather themselves before you continue. If the deep breathing didn't do the trick, taking a sip of water can be enough to break that emotion. If you used a symbol on your notes, focus on the symbol while you pause. Once you are ready continue with the eulogy.

After the service has concluded, be prepared for people to approach you. If you need a moment to gather yourself, find a quiet place. From my experience, people will want to thank you for your words, comment about something that was said or share their own story. It can be quite overwhelming and I find taking a few moments for yourself is necessary.

Action: Practice delivering the eulogy.

Practice the eulogy, using your notes.

- o Use large font.

- o Use double spacing or 1 ½ spacing.

- Start each sentence on a new line.

- Add an extra line between paragraphs.

- Number each of the pages.

- Print single sided.

- Place all pages on the right-hand side of the lectern.

- As you near the end of the page, slowly move the page to the left.

- As you read your speech, lift your eyes regularly to make contact with the audience.

- Use your finger as a guide.

- Practice reading the speech and lifting your eyes.

Action: Deliver the eulogy.

- Pack your notes.
- Bring water.
- Bring a small packet of tissues.
- Arrive early.
- Introduce yourself to the person leading the service.
- Take a moment for yourself.
- Familiarise yourself with the speaking area.
- Stand behind the lectern and look at the room.
- Secure a seat with easy access to the speaking area.
- Deliver the eulogy when called.

A final word on bringing it all together

Take time for you, take time to breathe and remember who you are doing this for.

Blessings to you as you speak from the heart with tears.

From the Heart with Tears

CHAPTER 5

Finding Inspiration

Turn your hurt into healing, your wounds into wisdom and your pain into power.
ROBIN SHARMA

✦ ✦ ✦

I often find that the stories from family members inspire me however I also find meditating and consulting the amazing world of the internet helpful. I have found that this helps me in many ways, including to:

- process my own grief
- find the right words, and
- draw strength to do the eulogy.

I have found inspiration in poems, quotes and songs over the years. Here is a sample of sources of inspiration for me:

- The Star by Catherine Turner
- I Felt an Angel by unknown author
- Gone Fishin' by Delmar Pepper
- Irish Blessing by Anon
- Footprints in the Sand by Mary Fishback Powers
- As We Look Back by Clare Jones
- When I Must Leave by Helen Steiner Rice

- o Death Is Nothing At All by Henry Scott-Holland

- o Remember Me by Margaret Mead

- o Farewell My Friends by Rabindranath Tagore

- o (Everything I Do) I Do It For You by Bryan Adams

A final word on finding inspiration

You can find inspiration from others and from the internet, however I believe the greatest inspiration comes from within. You have the magic within you, draw on yourself for inspiration.

From the Heart with Tears

Afterword

*Don't cry because it's over,
smile because it happened.*
DR SEUSS

✦ ✦ ✦

You have been given an opportunity that most people would refuse. By following this simple process, you will be able to honour your loved one while providing comfort to their family and friends.

It takes a special person to say "yes" and when you take a moment to reflect on what you have done, appreciate the gift you have given and be proud.

Blessing to you as you speak from the heart with tears

Kaylene

From the Heart with Tears

About the author

Kaylene Ledgar is on a mission to erase the fear of speaking. Kaylene says "You don't need to fear speaking; speaking is a learned skill and you can master it."

16 years ago, Kaylene made the life-changing decision to face her fear of speaking. Fear of speaking used to consume her, but now with hundreds of speaking opportunities under her belt, she is a motivational speaker who helps others to overcome their fear of speaking. Kaylene shares tips and tools to overcome the fear of speaking in her book Speaking, It's NOT Worse Than Death.

Kaylene believes that when our actions match our values, we unlock our true path. In 2019, she decided to close the door on her 26 years career in the Australian Public Service to be a full-time coach, speaker and live her true path.

Kaylene is a certified World Class Speaking Coach and certified Holistic Life, Career and Executive Coach. She has a Diploma of Government - Management and Certificate IV Training and Assessment. She has been a member of Toastmasters International for 16 years, regularly volunteering for leadership roles at Club and District levels.

Kaylene is the eldest child of David and Lavinia, sister to John and David, and mother to her two cats, Dream and Magic. After 16 years living interstate, Kaylene has recently returned home to Frankston South, Victoria, Australia.

Kaylene can be contacted through her website:

www.kayleneledgar.com.au

About the author

www.ingramcontent.com/pod-product-compliance
Lightning Source LLC
Chambersburg PA
CBHW021133080526
44587CB00012B/1273